John Re

KEEPER OF

THE

MEMORIES

John Regan

Published in Hardback, 2023, in association with: JV Author Services
www.jvauthorservices.co.uk
jvpublishing@yahoo.com

ISBN: 9798851775055

FOREWORD

This book represents the poems I have written over the previous fifteen years. The majority, however, have been written in the last six.

I have grouped the poems according to the subjects they describe, allowing the reader to quickly find a subject. Whenever I have bought and read poetry books, I have always liked the difference the turning of a page can bring.

I hope some of these poems resonate and, in reading, you take something from them.

John Regan, 2023.

Find me on Facebook and Instagram.
John Regan – Author
Email – johnregan1965@yahoo.co.uk

DEDICATION

This book is dedicated to the memory of Dean Gilligan. A friend and work colleague who sadly had to leave the party when it was still in full swing. A poem I wrote for Dean can be found on page 9.

John Regan

LOSS

We miss people, and we, in turn, will one day be missed by others.

ALL OF YOU

Within the shadows of my mind
There blooms a flower bright and true
Which wears a coat that you once wore
And shimmers still in time anew

Occasionally, I visit there
To smell the fragrance I once knew
And gaze upon the thing once held
Encapsulating all of you

Enjoy Life's journey. We won't be here forever.

LIFE

Nothing lasts forever, not even the earth and
sky
So let's be joyous while we walk this way
For all your money, won't another minute buy
Nor gold a dawning of a newborn day

A poem in celebration of the wonderful work the NHS staff and care staff continue to do throughout this crisis and beyond. But also in memory of those workers who paid the ultimate sacrifice in their battle with this awful virus.

BENEATH THE ANGEL'S HANDS

Beneath the angel's hands, the stricken hover
And hope with break of morn they'll view new light
Their shallow breath forestalled in painful battle
Then thread-like hung in tenuous fight

Attendant-masked and apron-clad caregivers
Stare down the barrel of a pitiless foe
But carry on in effort at deliverance
And slow the march of deathly blow

Though helplessly, we look on at these selfless guardians
We see the price which some were asked to pay
When earthly wings, unfurled, stretched-tight, unfolded
And life took flight on dark and sombre day

John Regan

In memory of a friend and work colleague

THE THING I'LL MISS THE MOST

It's the smile I'll miss the most
And that sense of humour too
Your glass-half-full philosophy
Your genuine through and through

The stories you would tell me
About the characters you had known
Your love for all things animal
Your Joop Jump spray cologne

The love for all your family
The grandkids were your light
The love for your wife and children
Which always shone so bright

I'll miss when I used to run into you
Our chance to reminiscence
I'll miss your colourful stories
I'll miss your take the piss

I'll miss your larger-than-life persona
I'll miss my welcome host
But it's the smile and sense of humour
That I'll really miss the most

When you feel like giving up, remember the reasons you've stayed this long. The people who love you will never recover from your loss.

THE ECHOES OF THE SOUND OF YOU

How black does darkness need to be
To dowse the light of life's great call
How deep despair or sadness plea
That plunges long in hopeless fall

What causes those to cast aside
And give up hope in reckless blow
Then set in motion deathly slide
Which gathers speed in rapid flow

Did pain and kin reign over you
Enticing you down sorrow's well
In growing trope of darkest blue
Encased in walls of baleful cell

If only you had glimpsed the hand
That stretched so hard to pull you through
It might have drowned out death's demand
In ardent pure, and fervent coup

You may have found the strength to fight
And battled on in day renew

Then headed back towards the light
With steadfast soul and passion too

But you were lost in setting-sun
Your demons grew in might and power
They masked the joy you could have won
And led you to that final hour

Those left behind enduring long
Reflect on what they would have done
Now understand your mournful song
And feel the pain of life which stung

There is a place remaining still
Inside of hearts of people who
Are left to view the ground now chill
Which echoes with the sound of you

Sometimes life can be difficult to traverse

DARKNESS

At the height of my distraction, I was blindsided
by the fall
Which screamed for my attention in a deafening,
relentless call
And dragged from my quiescence, I was
humbled on my knees
In the darkest forest I had known, beneath the
stygian trees
A land where none would wish to live, in a realm
that all should dread
Subsumed with loss and wanting in a place
where hope has fled

Unfortunately, Some memories are destined never to be written, but they live out there somewhere.

THE EMPTY SEAT OF MEMORIES

The empty seat of memories
Sits quietly in the shade
Beneath the bough of longing
In time's eternal glade

And ghosts of words unwritten
Drift gently in the breeze
Around the land of reverie
In never-ending frieze

The orphan and its kith and kin
Wait silently in hope
In company of might have been
Played out in sadness trope

A kiss of breath that could ignite
The liberty of speech
Is cast adrift on endless seas
And just beyond our reach

For Dad – 1932–2020

GONE BUT NOT FORGOTTEN

The echoes still reverberate through time's eternal sea
With memories that coruscate in thoughts of you and me

From childhood reminiscences down adult memory lane
To boyhood evocation and adulthood refrain

For death has no dominion and cannot hope to hold
A love once cast from life itself then dipped in purest gold

Losing our soulmate means we alone must carry the memories we once shared.

KEEPER OF THE MEMORIES

The double-edged sword of remembrance
The painful weight I hold
My torture and my torment
My priceless piece of gold

Those beautiful reminiscences
That heavy cross to bear
Alone in isolation
With no lost love to share

I am the sole keeper of these memories now
They were ours, but now they're mine
Recumbent with what could have been
Cast adrift within your shrine

The land where smiles exuded
Forever cast in black
No forward-facing marching on
Just always looking back

The stab, the sting which seeks me out
A heart deep-scarred, embossed
Is shattered now in fruitless search
For everything I've lost

A look through our phone contacts will include people we have lost but whose numbers we can't bear to delete.

LEFT UNDELETED

I haven't taken you out of my contacts
It's something I can't bear to do
All those texts and calls that we shared long ago
Remind me of what we once knew

I foolishly think you may ring me
From a galaxy far, far away
Where synapses and neurons still fire out new words
And your axons continue their play

I haven't deleted your number
But there might come a time when I do
And for now, you reside in my mobile
Just because it reminds me of you

When you feel like giving up, remember why you held on so long.

LIFETIME'S PAIN

Did deep despair accompany you
Through stygian lands, 'neath darkest blue
While hurt and pain, and loss accrue
Which beckoned on unwelcome coup

Great height that left you broke and small
Enveloped high behind closed wall
In sight of deathly face and sprawl
Then cast you down in endless fall

And did you beg and plead and pray
For happiness and joyful stray
When sand ran out on final day
As lifetime's pain just ebbed away

A poem about losing my dad.

MY BLUEST SKY

My bluest sky has lost its glow
As curtain falls across the stage
And silence reigns forevermore
On turning of the final page

And drenched in dread, I viewed this day
With hope, I would be left unbowed
But only now I feel the loss
Loom large in dark foreboding cloud

Yet I will walk on memory lane
Beside the man I called my dad
Along the road that once we owned
Within the land of time we had

And I will often raise a smile
With recollections, I'll compart
Steadfastly held in safest place
Wrapped up with love within my heart

John Regan

The Queen's Funeral

STATELY PAGEANTRY

Prepare the stately pageantry
And set the flags half-mast
Then put aside tomorrow
And dwell upon the past

Prepare the canons far and wide
While a nation rendered mute
Stands silently in reverie
In one last royal salute

Make ready the regal retinue
Silence the people's shout
Saddle up the horsemen
And let the bells peal out

Then gather up the dignitaries
As grief and the sadness fall
For the passing of her majesty
And her final curtain call

Losing someone radically changes our lives.

LIFE AND LOSS

You haven't lived until you've lost
Only then can you comprehend
How life lays bare at sullen cost
The bitterness of the end

Our grief then measured in teardrops
As loss joins force with pain
In mournful ache which never stops
And sings its sad refrain

A painful lesson quickly made
Will forever stain and mar
A sharp awareness swiftly weighed
Of how precious our loved ones are

When those memories of your mother arrive unexpectedly

THE GHOST OF YOUR SMILE

The ghost of your smile came from out of the blue
Tugging softly on strings with a sadness anew
And I willingly drifted in a land we once knew
To a place that's replete with the essence of you

The sound of your voice and a touch almost real
Feel light years away from that final appeal
But the hurt and the loss I fight hard to conceal
Are dwarfed by the love that I'll gladly reveal

And time, even stretched, is never a dam
If held to account in my thoughts which will cram
When counting my debt owed from adult to pram
Wrapped up in my memories and thoughts of my mam

Those boxes, full of memories – we can't bear to part with – of people we have lost.

YOU ONLY LIVE IN BOXES

You only live in boxes now
When once you shone so bright
You only live in boxes now
Away from lifetimes light

You only live in gilded frames
Behind a piece of glass
That hangs on walls or sits on shelf
As months and years bypass

You only live in memories now
Which stab and haunt and sting
That brings to mind what I have lost
And will forever cling

You only live in boxes now
And there you must remain
Until I find the strength I need
To visit you again

I felt compelled to write this poem after passing through a cemetery and seeing a young mother knelt at the grave of a young child. The headstone surrounded by flowers and balloons.

THE HEAVY HEAD OF LOSS

Oh, heavy hangs the head of loss
Which lives and breathes on sombre road
Asleep beneath a painful cross
A grievous and a ponderous load

But like a moth, I'm drawn to you
And all that waits is sorrow, long
I can't resist the flame once knew
Where future drowned in mournful song

Though adulthood was my abode
And childhood smile now solace flown
You never passed from infant road
With tragic seeds of life unsown

A poem about my father-in-law – a proud Yorkshireman – and some of the things he loved.

BELOVED YORKSHIRE ROSE

Scatter me beneath blue sky, below a sward of darkest green.
Where I will dance with summer sun and bask in warmth of soft, serene
And lay my soul in earthly bed, and boundless sleep will cushion me
From life's travails and care's unrest, now lifetime bonds have set me free
Where pain and suffering are shed, and memories drift on endlessly
Towards a countless span of time, to live on now eternally
For I, with luck, have lived a life in umbra of the brightest rays
On bluebell carpets, I have walked in autumn light and springtime days
I think of journeys I have made through golden fields or floral parks
With canine family long since gone, I still recall their playful barks
Watched willow firm and leather, too, meet fast in thrall at Headingley
Seen untold boundaries cross the line and overs bowled in proudest glee

Or watched as oval passed from hands, of burly
prop to hooker stout
I cheered on Lions decked in red, or men in
white with nation rout
I brought the spark of light to some, illuminating
far and wide
With softly spoken words of sage, I watched on
in paternal pride
Although my body failed in time and cast adrift,
it kept me chained
My daughter's Grand, who stole my heart, the
adoration never waned
In crossword puzzles, we would joy or music in
the jazz I knew
They kept alive a trace within, which never
wandered from the true
But now my days have run their course, and
close of play has come to pass
I shut my eyes one final time below my bed of
greenest grass
I'll stay with you and rest a while, and there I'll
sit in quiet repose
In shadow of my rose-topped hill, beneath my
beloved Yorkshire rose

LOVE

Dedicated to my wife. A poem about the importance of love.

LOVE

Bright light in sunshine glow will lift the heart
But dark will not a stranger stay
As grains of time pass by unknowingly
Sweet life is lent the essence of another day
Yet those that grasp within their hands the minutes held in love
And view these as sagacious deed
Then wonder why they toiled in other fruitless realms
While sits before their seeing eyes
Entirety of all they ever need

If you can learn to love yourself, loving other people comes easy

YOU

Don't take yourself too seriously
It'll only end in tears
Or beat yourself up over trivial things
And be hostage to all your fears

It's what's inside that really counts
Isn't that what they say
Be brave, ignore the jibes
And face that new-born day

Don't be a second-rate version
A poor copy of those you admire
There's only one person you need to impress
A someone you need to aspire

You've spent all your life in their company
You've laughed, and you've cried with them too
They know every dream that you'll ever possess
The person you need is called you.

Dogs, you've got to love them.

BEST FRIEND

Tell me a secret that only you know
I promise to keep it and never let go
Tell me you want me and show me you care
I'll love you forever and always be there

I'll forgive your transgressions, your
wrongdoings, too
I'll be faithful and loyal, and I'll always be true
Lift spirits on days when you're sad and feel
down
Put a smile on your face when I act like a
clown

I'll come running to you, just give me a shout
I'm pleased when you come home, of this you
won't doubt
All I ask in return is really quite small
Some food, a walk and maybe a ball

We all need that special someone we can rely on.

I WANT YOU THERE

I want you there when the sky falls in, when the sea crashes down, and my world starts to spin. I want you there by my side in the face of the tide of uncertainty.

I want you there when the darkness descends, when my courage has failed, and I've lost all my friends. I want your arms wrapped around when my hope has all drowned in a sea of doubt

I want you there hand in hand when all others have gone, and I'm making a stand. I want to bask in your warmth when the light is no more than a flicker in the distance of some faraway shore

I want you there at the end when the curtain has fell and my last words are penned. I want your voice to echo loud when my spirit is bowed, and the essence of life is no more.

HOPE

Never give up hope. Never.

HOPE

When darkest nights are all you own
And sunshine never comes to stay
The time limps by with leaden feet
Grey clouds possess the gloomy day

And you could drown in deep despair
Watch walls close in around your head
Give up the fight, accept defeat
And curl up tight in sombre dread

But maybe there is something still
The lifeline and a safety rope
That lives within the inky black
And shines the beacon we call hope

Our hopes, dreams and aspirations live out there somewhere. We just have to seek them out.

HOPES AND DREAMS

Beneath the wings of spiritual things
Within the touch of new-born hands
Within the sight of loving eyes
Beneath the sun in untrod lands
Where aspirations flow like streams
And time stands still, or so it seems
Where we might hear occasionally
The echoes of our hopes and dreams

Imagining a place where we're all a little more equal.

PROMISED LAND

I glimpsed a sight of something grand
Beyond dark hills and sullen sky
A song so sweet which sang to me
My soul let out a deafening sigh

A place where beds aren't made of stone
And innocence not left to lie
On hardest floors of callousness
Or aged past pushed out to die

Where banks of food aren't piled up high
Or those that served, forgotten too
And everyone can feast on hope
A time of many, and not the few

And if I stumbled on my path
There'd be someone to lend a hand
To help a heart which beats like theirs
And carry me to promised land

NATURE

Get ready for the year's most colourful season.

AUTUMN

We lift our heads in reverence
When every leaf is a flower
In shades of orange, red and brown
Subsumed in autumn's power

The mosaic of all seasons
When summer waves goodbye
We've lost the blooms but gained the fruit
As wintertime stands nigh

Has nature saved these gems for us?
In pocket-laden gold
The year's last smile of loveliness
Is ours to behold

How beautiful the leaves grow old
Within their final days
As jewels float down from lofty trees
In summer's final blaze

A host of golden daffodils

DAFFODILS

With gilded kissed magnificence, they quickly
bring
Bright golden-coloured loveliness that heralds
spring
In multitude and numbers much greater than
before
A wave of sunshine beauty bathes our greenest
shore
As if the sun itself had crept down from above
Then showered fast the lawns and hedgerows
with its love
But while this fleeting star does not, the summer
make
True excellence is set for those that follow in
their wake

As Covid played out, nature carried on as usual.

THE BIRDS DON'T CARE

The birds don't care that we're not there to hear
their tuneful song
They flit from tree in life carefree within their
feathery throng
The bees are blind, and they don't mind if we
aren't there to see
They kiss the flower and dance through bower
in sunny patch or tree

The tiny ant has feeling scant cares nought of
how we fare
They build their homes beneath cold stones
away from human stare
All nature, too, with wondrous hue ignoring
humanity's plight
She carries on in glorious song, knowing
nothing of our fight

How many green and beautiful spaces have been lost to the relentless march of modernity?

WHEN FIELDS WERE GREEN

I remember when those fields were green
And nature shone with sparkling hue
Where flora danced with wondrous pomp
With every kind of fauna too

I remember when the trees stood tall
And bent their heads in autumn breeze
A sea of amber that stretched forever
Then glistened bright in winter freeze

I remember when beguiling views
Would stretch for miles in vista long
And days great call prolonged in time
The company of new birdsong

But then, from ground, grew red and grey
And swallowed up the meadows old
Then swept aside the centuries past
And carried off all nature's gold

After winter, the welcome sight of spring.

WONDEROUS SPRING

As soft white motes drift softly down
And gently gather at my feet
I cast my mind to mellow realms
Which rise and stretch in timely greet

Oh, how I've missed your temperate smile
That sweet caress from warmer hands
To walk again down milder lanes
Beneath the sun of longed-for lands

A time of joy, where life erupts
And all of nature starts to sing
I hear the sound and smell the scent
That beckons in the wondrous spring

John Regan

The beautiful sight that erupts each year

BLUEBELL WOOD

Through woodland realms and sunny ways, I walk in tiptoe true

Atop a carpet stretched for days in ocean-covered blue

I pause a while, in awe-struck time and drink in nature's hue

Transfixed in silent reverie within this wondrous view

Mother Nature might not put up with us forever!

THE COMING DAWN

Infest the land, fill up the sea
And strip the earth in greed's decree
Ignore the cost and looming fee
As deafness reigns despite some plea

Yet mother, when she has a mind
Won't look away forever blind
Fast plummet deep in holes we mined
Then forced to pay the bill we signed

In coming dawn, we least suspect
Life moribund and bloody-flecked
Will lead in time to headway checked
Where future's child lies lost and wrecked

Those beautiful Spring-like mornings

SUNLIGHT

An icing-coated morning shone
And sunshine wore a spring-like dawn
As I drew in a welcome breath
I thanked the stars that I was born

Watching as the little bird feeds her chicks

THE LITTLE BIRD

Through tracery, I watch her dart
In swiftness heat past blinking sun
Then dance within the fallen leaves
Amongst detritus, windswept spun

Then up again to lofty tree
She pirouettes with captured prize
To waiting young, ensconced in roost
Who call to her in plaintive cries

Then back to wing, she takes to flight
Relentless in this endless chain
From canopy to leafy shore
From leafy shore and back again

John Regan

WAR

Warring people and nations claim to have God on their side.

MY GOD IS BIGGER THAN YOUR GOD

Shall we sing a funeral dirge
for the Gods who have passed this way
Who withered and died, then slipped from our grasp
Buried deep in the moral decay
And the Angels and heavenly choirs
Did they stow away their feathery wings
Then moved to a place where the fighting had ceased
In a land far away from the kings
Were holy books traded for Kalashnikovs
Along with a Faustian pact
While sense and reason were jettisoned
And exchanged for something abstract
Did they give up their lifetime and opportunity
With a contract they signed for in blood
From people who suffered injustice
Then drowned in their ensuing flood
My God is bigger than your God
Was the zealot's clarion call
They burned at the stake all the heretics
While praying for their enemy's downfall
Did they view all the killing as trivial
The collateral damage of belief

As the bodies piled high on the altar of loss
Did they ignore the great ocean of grief
If these gods really ever existed
They would view men's work with a smile
Shake their heads in collective repugnance
Then set up their court for a trial

A poem in remembrance of those who gave up their lives for us in numerous conflicts.

IN BLOODY FIELDS

On bloody fields in deathly land
As clock ticked past eleventh hour
The madness that had held them firm
Was left to taste the sickly sour

And silence grew from deafening guns
Which drew to close the carnage long
The ghosts of lost lay restful down
Beneath the sound of new birdsong

Erected in the farthest shires
Bedecked in brass on monument
That marked the depth of nation's loss
In every squad and regiment

And seats in homes lay empty, then
No voice to echo around the room
Or touch from hands forever gone
Just sepia past to aid their gloom

So now we view this fallen kind
As martyrs and the hero ranks
And wear a flower of crimson hue
With reverence and heartfelt thanks

It's politicians that cause wars, but the innocent people who have to bear the consequences.

THE FORGOTTEN, THE WOUNDED AND LOST

The tears will fall like rain from the sky into a
bottomless ocean of grief
And faces that laughed and smiled months
before are robbed of this smile by a thief
Crushed under the tracks of an unjust war, they
are rendered no more than a number
As they pass from the living to premature end
and a timeless and permanent slumber
When the rich wage their wars, it's the poor that
will pay, for its greed and avarice which win
And as death marks the time and then sharpens
his scythe, politicians will casually spin
For truth is the first victim of war, along with the
forgotten, the wounded and lost
And the tyrants ignore all the rivers of tears, the
suffering, the pain and the cost

John Regan

MEMORIES

Those wonderful memories arrive from nowhere and take you back to a place in time before disappearing again.

MEMORIES ARE MADE OF THIS

That longed-for moment filled with charms
On temporal dawn, through timeless glee
Fast rests within my welcome arms
Then resonates, a part of me

On wings of speed, you sought me out
With past remind, I'd long forgot
And like a bolt, I'm joined in rout
In memory bright, and warm besot

Let's dance a while, as moment lasts
And bathe within the sea of time
Then reminisce in homily
'til life rings out quotidian chime

Memories are strange things. Over time the recollection of the event is altered so that your memory from the past hardly resembles what happened. But does it matter? As long as we retain a vague outline.

THE VAGUEST OUTLINE

As shadows take shape, I gaze backwards at you
A lifetime in years dressed with memories accrue
And faces I walked with drift back into view
Then gleam in a country of places we knew

This presence made real, and a touch of a hand
Emotions and feelings are scattered and fanned
Left rooted and struck, lost in time, here I stand
In this place where my heart will always crash-land

But my youthful coat that I wore now is cast
The snow filled my hair as the time galloped past
And cracks in the walls grew and quickly amassed
Maybe these memories of mine are miscast

As time chips away at my yesterday wall
The writing once crystal is rendered in scrawl
And the long-ago story is flimsy and tall

As certainties shake and then finally fall

But then, does it matter if the stars don't align
And my once recollections don't shimmer or shine
For thoughts of the past are unique, and they're mine
As long as I cling to the vaguest outline

Although we find ourselves occasionally looking back longingly at our youth, there are benefits to growing older.

THE ESSENCE OF YOU

The essence of you lingers
In stairways, rooms and halls
When once they echoed loudly
To those long-ago footfalls

I see a face still smiling
From that one-time lived-in land
I feel the vernal heartbeat
And a touch of youthful hands

Somewhere deep within me
Lives all you ever were
I loiter close occasionally
And briefly pause to stare

Although I miss those bygone years
From time to time with age
I love the wisdom I have gained
With every turning page

**The child we once were has not disappeared;
it is buried deep inside us. Occasionally,
though, we glimpse our younger selves and
smile knowingly.**

THE SILHOUETTE OF ME

As I gaze through distant shadows
And watch the years pass-through
I see a face I recognise
The silhouette of you
But once I lived behind that smile
And dreamed of unknown lands
My youthful coat, I wore with pride
Shone brightly in my hands
Although the snow has covered
The rooftop and the tree
The thoughts I kept of yesterday
Are buried deep in me
But now and then, they surface
From time's remotest well
And bring to mind the memories
Of where my footsteps fell

John Regan

HUMOUR

Inspired by a friend of mine who has a chubby cat called Duncan.

DUNCAN'S DAY

Duncan, the cat, was so very fat
The vet said he had to lose weight
His owner decreed; she'd put an end to his greed
When he struggled to fit through the gate
He got lodged in a fence with his body so dense
she decided a diet would work
But he was one step ahead when she popped off
to bed
With a swish of his tail and a smirk
He recruited a friend with money to spend and a
cat flap not far away
Now the pair of them feast like a couple of
beasts and sleep off their excess all day.

A bit of fun surrounding food and drink.

IF I WERE A CAKE

If I were a cake, I would be an éclair
With that choux pastry essence and a certain
savoir-faire
That luscious chocolate covering and the cream
through and through
So, I wouldn't be a vanilla slice or a lemon
drizzle too

If I were a cool drink, I'd be a shandy bass
Not a lemonade, or an iron brew, they lack a
certain class
With half per cent of alcohol, I'd be the king of
the pop
No other brand or type of drink would make
me want to swap

If I were a lolly, I'd be a cider one
There's nothing better for licking when you're
sitting in the sun
You can keep your strawberry mivvi. and your
sprinkle-covered fab
The cider-flavoured lolly is the one that I
would grab

If I were a pudding, I'd be a spotted dick

Cover me in custard; that would really do the
trick
There are lots of other foodstuffs that I would
like to share
But my dinner's almost ready, so I'm going to
leave it there.

Toys had to be tough in my household.

BROKEN TOYS

I had a Tonka toy when I was a boy
Almost Indestructible, the makers said
I hit it with a Hammer, a mallet and a brick
And buried it next to the shed

I got a Stretch Armstrong for Christmas
And stretched and pulled him with pride
But when it was time to re-box Stretch
I had to fold him to get him inside

I loved my Hornby model train set
I reenacted a John Wayne scene
Where the engine rushed by in the blink of an
eye
Then careered off a mighty ravine

I'm sorry I mistreated my toys back then
And I still feel quite guilty today
I wish I cared for them better than I did
When I see what they fetch on eBay

Is Mother Nature deliberately producing rude fruit?

NAUGHTY FRUIT

Consider the banana; why is it that shape?
Couldn't it be roundish, like an orange or a grape?
With its priapic appearance and its breezy savoir-faire
Its sunny disposition and its easy-peel affair

Could it be that Evolution has a sense of humour too?
And we are left oblivious without a single clue
We carry on regardless and accept things as they are
No matter how unusual, no matter how bizarre

I think that Mother Nature is giggling at our expense
Then offers up this odd-shaped fruit with *'it's good for you'* pretence
And other fruits are just as rude if I may bang my drum
Like peaches, melons and kiwis and what about the plum!

A typical day in my household.

I'VE GOT A FAIRY AT THE FOOT OF MY GARDEN

I've got a fairy at the foot of my garden; I've
seen her when I look out of the door
I watch her whizz by in the blink of an eye in a
fluttery dance I adore
I've got a unicorn that lives in my attic; I can
hear it clomping about
It clippity clops, and it bumps, and it bangs; it's
making a mess, I've no doubt
I've got a Leprechaun under my floorboards; I
can hear when he curses and swears
He's probably looking for his pot of gold, but
I've hidden that under the stairs
But the funny thing which I have noticed is that
these creatures only ever appear
When I'm holding a glass full of wine or with
rum or after copious bottles of beers
I know what you're thinking on reading this, that
these creatures are not real at all
That I've just made them up out of thin air, and
the story I've told is quite tall
But I don't really care what you think of me; I'm
deaf to your heartfelt appeal
This is why I don't mind that I've owned up, and
it's why I would never conceal

That I do have a fairy in my garden, and when I
see her it makes me less glum
So I'll keep on drinking my beers, my red wine,
my port, and my rum

There are two things to remember about this poem. Firstly, you need a hole in your vest to put your head through. Secondly, I can't be held responsible for your dirty mind.

HOLE IN MY VEST

You're the hole in my vest and the sun in the sky
My first-morning glory, a wink of the eye

You're a large knob of butter on my warm toasted bread
A slip undercover in a freshly made bed

You're my know where the things are when I'm searching a drawer
And a nice piece of shag pile that covers my floor

You're a warm bowl of hotpot, a spicy, hot stew
A nice pickled gherkin, a well-fitting shoe

You're a partner in crime and part of my gang
A trumpet to blow and a drum I can bang

But most of all, gorgeous, you're my warm winter squeeze
A hole for my concrete; a baked Camembert cheese

A humorous Christmas poem.

SHOW ME YOUR BAUBLES

It's Christmas again, and what do you know
Some looking for cheer, some praying for snow
I'll show you my baubles if you show me yours
You can dress like an elf, and me, Santa Claus
I'll whip out my yule log; it's massive this year
I'll fondle your pudding and bribe you with beer.
I'll be stuffing your turkey like never before
Spit-roasting potatoes and banging the door
I'll be smearing on duck fat and cracking my nuts
Then getting my mouth around prime juicy cuts
Roasting the chestnuts while you flaunt your pie
I'll nibble your fondant and chew a bird's thigh
The table is groaning; it's got a full load
It won't take much more before I explode
And when it's all over, we'll sweep up the litter
Yank down the stockings, and whip off the glitter
Heave up my full sack and collapse on the floor
Look forward to next year to do it once more.

A bit of daftness

SHE, WHO SELLS SEASHELLS

Why didn't we know the name of she who sold
seashells on the seashore
Even Peter, who picked a peck of pickled
pepper, had a name
And Betty Botter, who bought some butter, was
name-checked just the same
Susie, who worked in a shoeshine shop where
she sat and shined some shoes
Had a lovely name to go along with her job, so
no one could ever confuse
I'm going to call her who sold seashells, Sharon.
I think this name will fit like a glove
So Sharon sold seashells on the seashore, so you
should ignore most of the above.
Come to think of it, wasn't it silly to sell
seashells on the seashore. Silly Sharon sold
seashells on the seashore, where there are
millions of the things she should have left them
on the seashore and learned to dance or sing.

The Sea Squirt really does exist, and yes, it does eat its own brain.

THE SEA SQUIRT

The juvenile sea squirt is a very curious thing
It travels on the ocean bed in search of a rock
to cling
When it finds the perfect one, it then devours
its brain
Certain in the knowledge that it won't need it
again

It's wonderful to think that a creature like this
exists
But less so if it stands on legs and frequently
insists
And if, in time, you've travelled through life's
relentless game
I'm sure, like me, you must have met some
people who've done the same

What's wrong with a good fry-up?

CEREAL KILLER

You're going to snap, crackle and pop when I
finally catch up with you
I'll wipe that Weetabix smile off your face and
that Special K countenance too
Your Sugar Puff clever demeanour and that
Shredded Wheaty chew
Will feel the force of my Frosties when I knock
your Alpen askew
I've put up with you all my life; I've gone Coco
Poppy too
Your Cheerios won't stand a chance, your
Cornflakes won't have a clue
Those stupid adverts, daft plastic toys and boxes
of every hue
And I'm sick of being dragged from my bed and
then having to look at you.

I worry about my memory.

FORGOTTEN

I remember everything,
Apart from the things I've forgot
I don't remember those at all
I've done this quite a lot

I'm hoping the things I remember
Are better than those I've forgot
I'm hoping the things not remembered
Aren't crucial to the plot

But what if the things I've forgotten
Are the most important of all
And all these things I've remembered
Are worthless and really quite small

Then I'd be left with useless memories
But nothing worth a share
I'd be oblivious to all I've forgotten
But I wouldn't really care

What if I don't remember writing this poem
And the web that I have spun
I would have to rely on Facebook
To remind me of what I've done

Messing about with nursery rhymes

JACK AND JILL

When Jack and Jill went up the hill to fetch a
pail of water, did they meet the Grand Old Duke
of York with his ten thousand men
Did they chat and smile pleasantly before they
went down again.
Maybe that's where Jack got his crown, the one
he broke, from the Grand old Duke, you see.
Maybe he stole it from the king when he had to
take the knee.
Maybe that's why he was going up the hill, to
get away from the king's men.
But if that's right, then why walk back down
again.
And whose idea was it to put the water up so
high. I can't help thinking that something had
gone awry.
When Jack fell, and Jill as well, and she came
tumbling after, where was the Duke of York,
neither up nor down.
Leaving Jack to mend his nob with paper that
was brown.
Oh, well, it goes to show that we should stay
away from hills, even if we need water, but
especially if we've got a crown.
Do the sensible thing and get your water from
the nearest town.

UPLIFTING

John Regan

The past, the present and the possible future.

THE FUTURE'S MINE TO OWN

I can't forget where I came from
Or the person I used to be
I can still see the footsteps I left far behind
That someone lives deep within me

Past echoes still resonate loudly
And the stars that shone still shine
As time edged its way to tomorrow
While planets accrete and align

As I sit in a place bathed in sunshine
In a land that has steadfastly grown
I can look to the past in a time I once held
And a future that's mine still to own

Those moments when you can ignore the hustle and bustle and enjoy living.

TAKING IT EASY

I'm taking it easy; I'm going for a stroll
I'm not reaching for targets or setting a goal
I'm watching the sunrise, easing into a chair
My worries are distant, out of earshot somewhere
I'm walking through sunsets, I'm browsing bookstores
I'm listening to blue seas that lap on our shores
I'm sipping a coffee, I'm resting my feet
There's no vital deadline that I need to meet
There's a bottle of red that I'm waiting to pour
And I'm holding on tight to the one I adore
Yes, I'm taking it easy, and there's no need to race
I'm ambling along in a wonderful place

Dedicated to anyone who is struggling to cope.

PAINT ON THAT SMILE

Paint on a smile; why not give it a try
I know that you're hurting, and you just want to cry
But I read in a book a long time ago
That sunshine and laughter can follow the snow

Paint on a smile, though you're dying inside
Your feelings can change, like the moon and the tide
Tomorrow might beckon, a day that is bright
And banish the sadness or darkest of night

Paint on a smile, and expel the blue
We are here if you need us; we're rooting for you
Remember the good times; the bad ones will fade
Remember the people, the reason you've stayed

Paint on a smile; why not give it a go
The highs that we long for can follow a low
Maybe our happiness is ours if we choose
Go on paint on that smile; you have nothing to lose.

John Regan

We can all be better people ... Can't we?

THE BETTER PART OF YOU

Put aside your prejudice
Ignore your bias too
Be colour-blind to humankind
And change your point of view

If you declare or even swear
To make your thoughts anew
You'll see mankind as one of us
And with your deeds be true

For if you can, you'll see the plan
That we can all push through
Within a place, a kinder face
The better part of you

John Regan

If you can learn to love yourself, loving other people comes easy

YOU

If you take yourself too seriously
It'll only end in tears
Or beat yourself up over trivial things
A hostage to all your fears

It's what's inside that really counts
Isn't that what they say
Be brave, ignore the jibes
And face that new-born day

Don't be a second-rate version
A poor copy of those you admire
There's only one person you need to impress
A someone you need to aspire

You've spent all your life in their company
You've laughed, and you've cried with them too
They know every dream that you'll ever possess
The person you need is called you.

LIFE

A New Year

THE NEW YEAR

In the mists of the morning
On the edge of dawn
Beyond the lunar dance
Another year is born

We'll look towards tomorrow
But think about today
Forget about what might have been
And cares that could outweigh

Cut fresh from time's eternal cake
A slice for us to own
It's ours to do with what we wish
Before the bird has flown

We hope this year is kind to us
So we can spend the time
Within the glow of those we love
Beyond the New Year's chime

We are born, and then we die. But in between? Who knows …?

THE ENDLESS SEA

A tiny drop of water in an endless sea
Plunged deep bereft of vesture on that day
Adrift amongst the riptides of adversity
Not knowing of the price I'd have to pay

Tossed high upon the hills of life's eternity
In brume and bosky countryside, I roamed
As living wore the lustre of uncertainty
And fortune owned the realm in which I combed

The echoes and the phantoms of what used to be
Inhumed within their once-remembered graves
At rest within a timeless long-forgotten lea
Still wreathe and lave in evanescent wave

In time what once was mine will fade in earthly
dust
This madding world and toilsome time will
shade
And light which shone so brightly fade in past
entrust
My spirit and my essence then unmade

We're not here long, so enjoy it.

ALONG FOR THE RIDE

Good morning to you, wherever you are
You got through the night, and you've made it
this far
Why not go for a walk or a dip in the sea
Stroll through a meadow or sip a nice tea

There will come a time when you live here no
more
And your footsteps have faded on life's sandy
shore
So while you're still here and along for the ride
Lift up your head and quicken your stride

**Rejoice in every new day. Eventually, we'll
run out of them.**

NEW BORN DAY

Deep slumber slips its dream-like chains
And wakefulness reclaims the realm
Of newborn day and earthly plains
Which ushers forth in virgin whelm

Then Helios, in golden dawn
Shines bright in splendid coruscate
A day held clear in wonder drawn
With freshness new on empty slate

And we should hold our precious gift
In knowing that there'll come a time
When joyous eyes and heartfelt lift
Will welcome in the final chime

Enjoy every minute, people. Old age is a journey not everybody gets to make.

THE JOURNEY

We wished away our childhoods
Though it's the greatest we'd ever feel
A brand new model straight out of the shop
And an energetic us at the wheel

We wished away those angst-ridden years
So we could legally drink
There was always a weekend over the hill
But they all flashed by in a blink

We wished away our twenties and thirties
Because we felt hard done or stressed
Money was tight, and life was a fight
With bills and chicks in the nest

Our forties were not any easier
With burgeoning kids to engage
We hoped they'd grow up and be happy
And enjoy each turn of the page

Our fifties were strangely relaxing
Most stresses we'd felt had now gone
We could stop for a while and take in a view
Smell the rose's before we strolled on

And if we live on till tomorrow
Where our golden years will reside
We should look on the time that we've spent
here on earth
As one great and incredible ride

Because old age is never a certainty
Of this, there can be no mistake
It's a journey that's full of more wondrous
things
But a journey, not all get to make

Treat every day as if it's your last.

LOVE MONDAYS

Don't disrespect Mondays or hate them so
much
because of their place in the week
They may lack the pull of a weekend day
Or a Thursday and Friday physique

But we need to remember how important they
are
and one thing we can't ever doubt
There will come a time in the future out there
where our Mondays will finally run out

Some days you're thankful for what you have.

BEAUTIFUL LIFE

Nothing lasts forever, not even the earth and sky
So let's be joyous while we walk this way
For all your money won't another minute buy
Nor gold a dawning of a newborn day

Chronic pain afflicts a lot of us. A constant companion we must learn to live with.

PAIN

In stygian realm of veiled reside
Of darkest days and blackest night
Where is this place in which you hide?
That fuels and boils with hate and spite

Oh, torture you have planned for me
In fervid joint or sinew sting
Beset my days and cloud my sight
With torment sharp, of pain you bring

The wax and wane can never fool
Your presence long, a lifetime spend
A penance for my younger days
will loiter long 'til bitter end

No sword have I with which to fight
Yet bete noir will not defeat
I'll battle on in strength resolve
With every breath and life heartbeat

We don't really know what the next day will bring. Happiness or sadness? Maybe we should treat these two imposters the same. Be happy, but not too much. And when sadness comes calling ... remember the good times may be waiting in the wings.

THOSE TWO IMPOSTERS

In lost horizons, I have trod
On summer's day or winter's night
Beyond my hopes, within my dreams
In darkest times or bright sunlight

I've tasted loss and felt the joy
Of life's travails or unknown lands
Which hide behind another day
Then touch our soul with unseen hands

For happiness, who wears a smile
And sadness with his coat of black
Walk hand in hand and next to us
Along an ever-winding track

Our only chance to still our heart
Or fail in haste to strike or blame
Is catch a breath and treat in type
Those two imposters just the same

There is nothing wrong with having hopes and dreams; everyone has them. But shouldn't we be happy and content with what we already have?

DREAMS

Our dreams are only borrowed from the library
of life
And history holds the hands of those that turned
the page
Of paragraphs and chapters of the long-
forgotten strife
Which echoes with remembrances of feet that
walked the stage

But if we give up on these dreams, content with
something less
It wouldn't bleach the colour leaving nothing
but the grey
If we can learn to understand the treasure we
possess
And view each virgin daybreak as our final
passing day

Memories of friends and drinking companions live on in the stories of those still here. One day, we, ourselves, will become the ghosts of the past.

THE LOCAL

Meet me where the pilgrims mass
Within the barrel mover's realm
With sunny cheer and fulsome glass
We gently drift and softly whelm
Where bibulous and dry imbibe
And bonhomie pervades the air
A tincture which we must subscribe
To briefly cast aside a care
Where ghosts of those who passed this way
Rub shoulders with corporeal kind
And sunk their last at close of play
Lived out in memories of those behind
Let's lift our hearts and down a beer
As time relentlessly pursues
For hid behind our fevered cheer
The battle which we all will lose

POLITICAL

Would the world be better if we weren't slaves to greed and capitalism?

CAPITALISM

Did capitalism die
Was it lost in twenty-twenty?
Did it breathe a last and final gasp?
Across the land of plenty

Is capitalism dead
Was it humbled on its knees?
Then coughed and spluttered and finally mourned
Despite the money men's pleas

Did capitalism die
Was it built on shifting sands?
A Machiavellian house of cards
In avaricious hands

Is capitalism dead
Was it buried beneath a lie?
Along with hollow promises
Beneath a Faustian sky

Social media can be a strange place. While one tragic event brings about an outpouring of emotion, another hardly causes a ripple. Just because people don't look or sound like us doesn't make it any less tragic. Or am I being foolish?

THE SUFFERING OF MAN

The opposite of love is indifference
And coldness hides the truth from sightless eyes
The words that tumble from the lips are worthless
As silence masks the sound of mournful cries

And those that look away from painful visions
Complicit in the actions of their clan
Cannot ignore the torment and the torture
Then claim to know the suffering of man

It is difficult to accept that our own opinions could be wrong, but other people's views were formed along an entirely different journey from ours.

OPINIONS

If I could see the world as you
And you could view the world as me
The chances are we'd still diverge
The odds are that we won't agree

Opinions held are nuanced-deep
And forged within our lives decree
We'd still retain those coverings earned
Which blind our eyes from what we see

If we don't fight to keep something, eventually, it will disappear

THE DEATH OF DEMOCRACY

Did you watch Democracy leave on the outward-bound gravy train
Waved it off ever so politely because you thought you wouldn't need it again
Did you manage to wrap up tightly, cover eyes with an ignorance cap
Jeered and cheered along with crowd, then started a slow handclap
Or did you pull high your collar of tolerance in an effort to keep out the chill
Of the icy-cold wind of indifference and the death of the once-held goodwill
Did you really think it immutable as you solemnly bid it goodbye
Did you lift up your hands, and cover your face, shed a tear and start to cry
Did you think, set in stone, that our system was really here to stay
That the laws of our land, and the people in power, would curb their own moral decay
Did you watch Democracy leave as it headed over the hill
With the rich and their pockets stuffed full with your cash, and you left holding their bill

Is it wrong to seek a better life for you and your family when only chance determines where we are born?

STROKE OF LUCK

I sat and watched the cork of hope
which bobbed upon the sea of life
Derided wide in breadth and scope
With bitterness, despite their strife

But surely we in fabled land
In thoughtful time that could be struck
Are mindful that our feet rest here
Is nothing but a stroke of luck.

The end couldn't come soon enough.

TAXI FOR JOHNSON

Taxi for Johnson, so off you trot. You've had all the time but never a plot
Go and do what you're good at and father more kids. You've been a crap prime minister; you're now on the skids
You drank booze and partied, then tried to advise. When we found out the extent, you still tried to lie
While people missed loved ones, funerals and wakes. You met with your friends and had drinks and cakes
So pack up your belongings and your suitcase of lies. Your acolytes, your light-weights and all your allies
We're not moving on until you do; your backbenchers hate you; they're plotting a coup
Go have some cheese and a nice glass of wine; you don't have to worry; you won't get a fine
Take all of your bluster and that silly blonde hair
You're going the same way as Thatcher and Blair
Yes, off you trot, Johnson; your time is now up
The nation has realised it purchased a pup

The Dunning-Kruger effect is where people tend to overestimate their ability or knowledge.

THE DUNNING-KRUGER EFFECT

I've read what you've posted, I've heard what you've said
I know most of the thoughts that float through your head
You're convinced your intelligence is higher than most
You do like to showcase; you do like to boast
But you're actually a dilettante with a superficial IQ
A walking bombast without any clue
Your bias and prejudice are easy to see
I doubt all your words, so we'll never agree
You opine, and you swagger, and what's more, I suspect
You're badly beset by the Dunning-Kruger effect

The Facebook and Instagram experts.

THE FOOLISH DENIERS

They won't be having the vaccine
or wearing a face mask too
That's what they say, the empty head clowns
The know-alls that haven't a clue

They're taking advice from some people
Like Hopkins, Farage and Graham
They're trawling the net for the fake news
Then fanning the anti-vax flames

They've seen a Professor from Kansas
Who swears he's a genuine Med
He's done all the sums and checked all those
stats
And there isn't a paper not read

They won't be having the needle
They've heard it can cause you some harm
There's someone they know who had it last
month
Now they've lost the use of their arm

They won't be having the vaccine
And they hope you won't have it too
They can't stand the thought that we're laughing
at them

'Cause they obviously haven't a clue

Oh, they won't be having that needle
And forget about wearing that mask
If they need any more information
There's a bloke from the pub they can ask

So, the next time you meet a denier
And they're trying to tell you they're right
You can roll your eyes or laugh in their face
Then tell them they're just talking shite

Could this really be the end?

THE END IS NIGH?

They're loosening up the restrictions
And the end is almost here
You can smell the local's home-cooked chips
You can almost taste the beer

You can meet outside with five others
If you can find five people you like
Stop avoiding the folk who get on your nerves
Spend company with those you dislike

You can get out your twenty-twenty body
The one you're ashamed of a smidge
And show everyone your achievement
By spending a year near a fridge

You'll be sliding the treadmill under the bed
The one with the cobwebs and dust
You'll be putting on eBay that exercise bike
It's already starting to rust

You'll be digging out the best of your carriers
The ones that cost 50p
You'll be filling the boot and the back of the car
In lieu of that first shopping spree

The gyms and the barbers are opening

You can flatten your abs and your hair
You already live in your joggers and sweats
So you won't hardly have to prepare

Oh, they're loosening up the restrictions
But it will never be the same
'Cause we lost twenty-twenty and people we loved
And we still don't know who to blame

You know the kind of people.

THE EGALITARIAN

I once knew an egalitarian; well, that is what he
claimed to be.
He would put a few coins in a beggar's hat or
buy them a cup of tea
He'd write cheques or pledge some money to the
lifeboat or homespun appeal
Put his grinning visage in front of a flag, and talk
of all wrongs with such zeal
But this person was only this generous if the
cause was the right one for him
If it wasn't, his unbiased principles would soon
lose their shine and then dim
Apparently, some people don't matter; their
colour or their creed rules them out
He didn't have time for the poor in the world,
for the starving or those lost in drought
He didn't mind that people were murdered at the
hands of a government somewhere
He couldn't invest all that sympathy; to be
honest, he just didn't care
Yes, I once met an egalitarian; he bought
poppies and daffodils too
But he didn't have time, and he never gave a
thought if they differed from me and from you

We all recognise this guy.

MR BLOVIATE

The colourful circus has pitched up in town,
along with a useless retinue
With acrobatic sophistry, hats of ambiguity, and
misinformation too
The big top clueless coterie funambulate the
narrowest wire
Then juggle half-truths endlessly while dodging
the crowd's cross-fire
And the ring-master in his coat of deceit causes
mayhem that has no bounds
He goes by Mr Bloviate, Liar in Chief,
duplicitous, King of all the Clowns.

Should and could the government have done more?

HEAVY HEART

Heavy hangs the head that wears the hubris
crown
But heavier is the heart which bears the pain
And all your empty rhetoric won't disavow
The part you played in ramping up the slain

Will history point a finger at your impotence
Which catalogued incompetence in multitude
Then understand the torment that you could
have stopped
And clearly see the light in which you should
be viewed

Social Media

THE LAND OF EMPTY RHETORIC

The land of empty rhetoric
Where idiots and fools opine
And truth is strangled in its crib
While button-tapping, nobodies whine

And spittle-mouthed who vent their spleen
Rain scorn on those who disagree
They stand behind a blind embankment
Enveloped in their lunacy

Their honesty and self-respect
Are left to feed on smallest scraps
While facts are pushed away with glee
And memories are left to lapse

The hypocrites and charlatans
Can fool a few but never stem
The well-informed and the erudite
Who see right through the lot of them

Another day, another mass shooting in America.

THE LAND OF THE FREE

In the land of the free and the star-spangled too
Constitution is law 'cross the red, white and blue
You can wave off your children and send them to die
In the briefest of moments, in the blink of an eye
Politicians are hamstrung; to arm is my right
And the lobby will win out because of its might
So, the lives of the innocent are measured in green
And the dollars stacked high until it's obscene
Drape the coffins with flags, then paint your world blue
In the home of the gun and the star-spangled too

COVID

What I imagined the first Lockdown would be like

CONTINGENCY PLAN

I'm going to build a castle of rum, with
battlements made of wine
And doors of every kind of beer, then treat it as
my shrine
If I can't go to pubs to drink, I'll make my home
a bar
And buy a still, fermenting kit, put whisky in the
jar

Break out the gin, tequila too, vodka, schnapps
and sake
Lock the doors and shut the blinds, then toss
aside the car key
I'll get out all the glasses I nicked from pubs
long ago
Hang up my Bass-Ale mirror, put the bar snacks
in a row

I'm dusting off my horse brass and my pewter
tankard too
The double diamond beer mats and cans of
special brew
I've even got surgical spirit; I'll add a dash of
lime

Drink scrumpy from a goblet, but never once call time

And when this hell is over, you can hang me out to dry
I'll be pickled like my onions and porky like my pies
Send a wagon for the empties when the Coronavirus tolls
Some bottles of hand sanitiser and a couple of toilet rolls

Because we all have friends and family we're missing right now.

UNTIL THAT TIME

Oh, distance etched with aching heart
Bereft of smile and kisses true
Missed hands once held that live apart
Your presence and your spirit too

A screen and voice cannot replace
This sad remote which we've become
Our life lived out in empty space
That leaves behind a feeling numb

But time's new light will one day fill
In strength resolve which did not wain
When grass grows green on future's hill
We'll meet en masse and laugh again

As panic buying took hold in early 2020, I decided to write a funny poem about people's obsession with hoarding toilet rolls.

MAKE YOU CRAP

The panickers were panicking, and the vacillators too.
This Covid 19 virus had the country in a stew.
But mild-mannered Billy Crabshaw was having none of it.
He'd read all the information, and it doesn't make you shit
'Why buy up all the toilet rolls?' he said to one poor soul
'Just keep your head, stop panicking, and have some self-control.'
'But what if what they've told us doesn't turn out right
And this Coronavirus really makes you shite?'
'You're mad,' cried Billy flatly. 'And off your chuffing head.
You've emptied all the biscuit aisle and half the bloody bread
The kitchen rolls, and handwash, Kleenex tissues too.'
He grabbed the man and shook his arm. 'It doesn't make you poo!'
'I don't believe the government; they talk a load of tripe

I don't intend to dither without a sheet to wipe.'
He waved a bony digit, fixing Billy with a stare
'You do what you want to, son.' And gave a
stubborn glare

He lifted high his toilet rolls, 'I bet I'm right,' he
cried
'I'll be wiping gleefully while you have to use
both sides.'

Billy glanced around the shop at others like this
bloke
And looked on rather helplessly at all these
manic folk

He pondered for a moment and gave his chin a
rub
What if this guy was accurate and shops ran out
of grub

He got a trolley, and then another, and then
another one
And shot off like a sprinter who'd heard the
starting gun

He started filling madly with anything in sight
Vim and Dettol and Mr Muscle and even Oven
Bright

'I'm having this, I'm having that, and some of
those,' he vowed
His trolley stacked so high by now; Dale Winton
would be proud

'Grab him,' screamed the manager. 'He can't
have anymore.'

But Billy just ignored him as he galloped around
the store
The shoppers couldn't stop him, nor the
checkout people too
Some stood and stared in disbelief as Billy's
shopping grew
He burst into the loading dock, past a startled
forklift driver
It never even dawned on Billy that he only had
a Fiver
The police were called, the army too, as Billy
ran amok,
It ended pretty badly when he tried to steal a
truck
He drove off in desperation and tried to make a
run
A vet nearby had to bring him down with a
tranquilliser gun
Now Billy sits in quarantine away from the
media glare
And dreams of owning Andrex while rocking in
his chair
A cause celeb they labelled him, the bloke that
went berserk
The family man, father of four, a mild-mannered
office clerk
Let this be a painful lesson, a salutary slap
It makes you sweat, it makes you cough, but it
doesn't make you CRAP!

The current state of play on social media.

IVORY TOWER

Look at you in the ivory tower
Just look how you glower
You're a denier, a liar, a bullshit buyer
Believing that crap, give yourself a backslap
Are you comfy in that echo chamber venting
your fury
Your own judge and jury
You're a snowflake hater, a woke slater
A conspiracy theorist, a flat-earther. A lack of
facts researcher.
A tinfoil helmet wearer, an Armageddon bearer
You're a right-wing lover, a fascist undercover
Daily Express supporter, a left-wing snorter
A Sun reader, a nonsense feeder, *hate all
foreigners* cheerleader
A Daily Mail kisser, an anti-establishment
hisser, an equality take the pisser.
You're a Johnson brown-noser, a common-
sense bulldozer
An egalitarian opposer
A transexual despiser, an anti-vax adviser, a
little-Britain Kaiser
A closet misogynist, a Farage and Tommy
Robinson enlist, a Katie Hopkins tryst
You're a climate change dismisser, a truth
avoider, an untruth embroider.

But in reality, you're a waste of space, a volte-
face, lacking any grace
A waste of good skin, a toss in the bin, a walking
talking chagrin
A living, breathing emetic, a human diuretic.
But most of all, you're pathetic.

John Regan

Could this really be the end?

THE END IS NIGH?

They're loosening up the restrictions
And the end is almost here
You can smell the local's home-cooked chips
You can almost taste the beer

You can meet outside with five others
If you can find five people you like
Stop avoiding the folk who get on your nerves
Spend company with those you dislike

You can get out your twenty-twenty body
The one you're ashamed of a smidge
And show everyone your achievement
By spending a year near a fridge

You'll be sliding the treadmill under the bed
The one with the cobwebs and dust
You'll be putting on eBay that exercise bike
It's already starting to rust

You'll be digging out the best of your carriers
The ones that cost 50p
You'll be filling the boot and the back of the car
In lieu of that first shopping spree

The gyms and the barbers are opening

You can flatten your abs and your hair
You already live in your joggers and sweats
So you won't hardly have to prepare

Oh, they're loosening up the restrictions
But it will never be the same
'Cause we lost twenty-twenty and people we
loved
And we still don't know who to blame

John Regan

Stay safe and keep your distance.

THIS SPACE BETWEEN US

This space between us seems to shout
We'll be all right if we just strive
To keep our moat and lone redoubt
The distance where we stay alive

VARIOUS

Dedicated to the lads who were brave enough to take the penalties during England's Euro shoot-out.

THE LONGEST WALK

On tenuous thread, does destiny hang
As dreaded failure sits and waits
For bell to chime in dolorous tone
And fearless souls to meet their fate

But there are those who sit and judge
When they have never walked that sward
And had to stare down mighty foes
Then raise up high their lion's sword

For those brave men who ventured forth
With nation's weight heaved high on back
Were stout enough to risk their all
And then stay valiant beneath the flak

The town where I live.

THE MIGHTY REDCAR

You wear your heart on your sleeve
Your scars and bruises were roughly born
Through ignorance and disregard
Past ridicule and scorn

Yet there within those glorious waves
Which dance across your sandy shore
Resides a future wide with scope
Where passionate people press for more

We'll beckon in a new-found hope
And watch the sun from sea-kissed plain
Then hold our breath with spirits high
Let mighty Redcar rise again

A poem I wrote for a friend of mine on his retirement. He is a singer and Deep Purple fan, so I decided to litter the poem with references to this.

THE COLOUR PURPLE

With guitar slung across his back, the minstrel
has left town.
To pastures new and untold heights, bedecked
with golden crown.
He leaves behind a legacy which money cannot
buy.
A cavalcade of memories, a silent battle cry.
To pastures new, a narrative that only he can
write
A storm to bring a sound to us and rock the
darkest night
We won't forget what we once had or fail to seek
it out
Rub shoulders with a Coverdale, of that I have
no doubt
If I were lucky in my life and lady dealer shone
on me
I'd meet a thousand perfect strangers on my
journey across the sea
But time has moods, and no one knows just
where this tale will end
I'll miss my kindred spirit, though; I'll miss my
purple friend.

Sometimes you just want to shut out the world.

MY LIFE AS AN ISLAND

I'm sometimes atrabilious
And often in a mood
Now and then I'm out of sorts
Occasionally I brood

My misanthropic tendencies
Extend to one and all
My antisocial arms-length stance
My high reclusive wall

No man is an island
Someone famous wrote
He maybe lacked my view on life
And didn't have my boat

Don't get stuck in your ways. There is so much more to learn.

THE ISLE OF IGNORANCE

Entrenched on isle of ignorance
We blindly face the sea
But dare we set a windward sail
And leave this blissful quay

Or do we turn our face away
Stuck fast within our lands
Content that all we need to know
Lives safely in our hands

But if out there, beyond our sight
Lies truth, and wisdom too
We'll miss the chance for us to learn
The things we never knew.

The lines, wrinkles and dark circles that now inhabit my face are a testament to the journey I have been on … The life I have lived.

TURN OFF THAT FILTER

We're all the same, but then again, we're all quite different in our own peculiar way
That's how it's always been and how it will always stay
Rejoice in those idiosyncrasies, your quirks and foibles too
It's who you are, it's who you've been, it's every bit of you
Stop filtering your photos on Facebook and Instagram; go for au naturel and not some counterfeit sham
We want to see the real you, not a veil or a mask
It's what people who love you would say; if you don't believe me, just ask
As Orwell said in a famous quote, 'We all get the face we deserve.'
That youthful glow that was ours long ago could never endure or preserve
Because our lifetime of trials and endurances, those losses and heartbreaks we faced
Are forever a huge piece of who we are and are now writ large and showcased

Most people are proud of where they come from. I'm no different.

TEESSIDE SOIL

The iron mined from earthly hill,
Which made the steel in rolling mill,
And built the ships with hands of skill,
And bridges far that tower still
Rests gently in my heart

And Marton boy that travelled far
Who mapped the world beneath the star
Crossed seas of green and land afar
Through ocean blue and sandy bar
Rests gently in my heart

The proud of Teesside born and bred
We hear the sound of time long-dead
Where giants walked and footsteps tread
Along the hills and riverbed
Rests gently in my heart

A Hercules was spoke in past
Where learned men and Peers massed
Those furnaces that fuelled and cast
While profits of a land amassed
Rests gently in my heart

Although a hundred years or more

Has quieted the ancient roar
We feel the past 'round town and shore
The hope to rise in new encore
Rests gently in my heart

The Erimus lion is not asleep
In watchful eye and castle keep
A harvest we will one day reap
Fraternity which runs long-deep
Rests gently in my heart

When time has shed my mortal coil
Emotions held no longer boil
And lifetime care has ceased the roil
I'll lay my head 'Neath Teesside soil
And gently rest my heart

The way celebrities are treated by the media and social media.

THE PROBLEM WITH CELEBRITY

Did you think it would be heaven and not this
hell
Tossing coins into your wishing well
Did you turn into a loser, not a winner
The wrong kind of sinner.
Have you passed all those people on the greasy
pole ascent
Only to slip back down when the drums began
their roll and celebrity came and went.
Did you suffer the Newtonian consequences of
pockets stuffed with cash
Were you sorry you acted rash
Did Brutus turn up with his dagger drawn, a
coup de gras which you helped spawn.
Are people in their own glasshouses pelting you
with stones and raking through your bones
Have you drowned in your contrition
Has your supernova dimmed
Has your lofty penthouse been vacated
And contracts quickly binned
Don't worry about the words being said
In a hundred years, we will all be dead
Next week your misdemeanours will be
wrapping up fish and chips

And another sun that shines so bright will suffer
a similar solar eclipse

John Regan

A poem about writing poetry!

RHYMING SYMMETRY

In countless hours I have toiled
In search of words to give me rhyme
On metaphors and similes
I've slowly chipped away at time

Looked endlessly and laboured long
On poetry or heartfelt verse
Wracked brains, lost sleep and given up
I've even caused myself to curse

In hot pursuit of life's mot juste
I've searched through books and internet
Re-written lines and jettisoned
And spent an age in thought, and yet

I love to see when I am through
And pleased I never chose to shirk
I battled on with doggedness
To finish up my lyric work

But even now I struggle more
To wheedle out and find that key
To bring an end to this short work
And win my rhyming symmetry

I was loaned an old postcard by a friend that had been originally posted in Middlesbrough in December 1914 by an unnamed gentleman to his sweetheart, Bessie. It is signed 'Your ever-loving boy.' I wrote this poem to try and evoke the emotions he was feeling.

FARMER BOY

My dearest Bessie, how I've dreamed
Your beauty shone on where I lay
I've yearned to take you by the hand
In walks through fields of golden hay

In meadows green in lambent light
I've viewed your face and flaxen hair
That wondrous smile which lights me up
And gazed upon your face so fair

Those eyes of viridescent hue
Which lifts my soul in endless joy
I hope your heart beats fervidly
And joins with mine, your farmer boy

Printed in Great Britain
by Amazon

42716771R00078